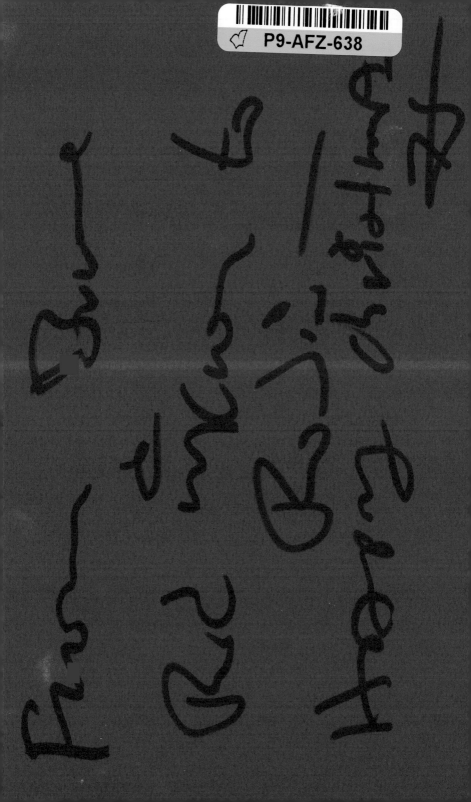

BOOKS BY ROD McKUEN

POETRY

AND AUTUMN CAME
STANYAN STREET AND OTHER SORROWS
LISTEN TO THE WARM
LONESOME CITIES
IN SOMEONE'S SHADOW
CAUGHT IN THE QUIET
FIELDS OF WONDER
BEYOND THE BOARDWALK
COME TO ME IN SILENCE
MOMENT TO MOMENT

COLLECTED POEMS

TWELVE YEARS OF CHRISTMAS
A MAN ALONE
WITH LOVE . . .
THE CAROLS OF CHRISTMAS
SEASONS IN THE SUN
AN OUTSTRETCHED HAND

COLLECTED LYRICS

NEW BALLADS
PASTORALE
THE SONGS OF ROD MCKUEN
GRAND TOUR

MOMENT TO MOMENT

moment
to moment

ROD McKUEN

CHEVAL
BOOKS
—
SIMON AND
SCHUSTER
—
NEW YORK

Part of the Holland section of this work was originally published
in the United States by Cheval Books in private edition, under
the same title. "Thursday" first appeared on the album *Rod McKuen/
Amsterdam Concert*. Other material has appeared in *Folio*.

This edition published by
Simon and Schuster
Rockefeller Center, 630 Fifth Avenue
New York, New York 10020
and
Cheval Books
8440 Santa Monica Blvd.
Los Angeles, California 90069
Manufactured in the United States of America

First printing September 1974

1 2 3 4 5 6 7 8 9 10

Library of Congress Cataloging in Publication Data

McKuen, Rod.
    Moment to moment.

    Poems.
    I. Title.
PS3525.A264M6 1974   811'.5'4   74-10780
ISBN 0-671-21839-5
ISBN 0-671-21921-9 (de luxe ed.)

Portrait of Rod McKuen on Binding by Romrey Ozalline

CONTENTS

AUTHOR'S NOTE

I have had small moments I thought big enough to coast on down a lifetime of unrest and no more love and there were epic times, or so I thought, that for some reason run no longer in my head no matter how much effort I put into their remembrance.

If I hadn't kept a diary—and that is what this is, a diary of two long goodbyes and maybe one hello mixed in—I'm not sure what would have stayed remembered and thus how much or little might have been made up. The re-creation sometimes turns out better than the fact. Because I felt these times important for myself, I rushed to write them down almost while they were happening.

I have published a book by this title twice before. The first was done privately and a second edition of that same book greatly revised was published last year in Great Britain by W. H. Allen. This volume contains less than one third of any of the poetry that appears in either of the previous books and some of the remaining poems have been revised sufficiently to make any comparison almost completely impossible.

The greater part of "A House by the Sea" was lived and written this year. With the exception of several poems that have appeared in the Christian Science Monitor, Woman's Day and Folio, none of the poetry in this section has been previously published. No part of the prose in either section of the book has seen print before.

Several of the poems are meant to be part of a much larger work about the sea, some of the prose is from The Word Went Out from Boston—a book in progress.

I have traveled to Holland yearly for a dozen years and yet what happened happened there in ten days' time. I have gone to Mexico every January for the past four years, each time coming home with a nearly finished book. I do not expect to visit Mexico again.

ROD McKUEN

April, 1974

Moment to moment each of us try
catching the cloud that holds back the sky ...
                                    McKuen

Holland, a diary—1971

For P. V. W.; who never was.

The Leaving

Lingering
as the dying do
between that life
　　　　　just past
and the still unknown,
I only know enough
about myself as yet
to know that I don't
　　　　　know enough.

Nor can I say
I know what's missing—
voids are voids
only seen completely
after we've had
victories over them.

I do not dangle
at the dawning
on a strand of sunlight,
nor do I perch on
paragraphs of prayers.
I'm hill and gully rider
only on the edge
of conversations
never in the center.

Get close enough to learn
but *lean* as little as you can
and only then
to have a closer listen.

All men have lessons
they can give you
even in rejection.
And the least
that you can offer
                any man
is your good arm
            or shoulder.

There will be
times when many
will want pieces of you
but only offer up the whole.

The small times count.
The inches not the miles.
Touches not tradition
will fill your memory
in the morning or the end.

And memories are
the only sanity
the world can now
                assure us.

While traversing a lifetime
we should not concern ourselves
          with steps that lead us
                    day to decade
or even year to year.
Moment to moment is enough,
you do not ask for more
though it is
          certain to be given almost always.

Whatever interlude
     of kindness or of light,
real or pretended
     you see coming
through the distance
be ready and be open.

The cost
of one warm moment
is considerable
but worth the poverty
that staying private means.

I know this and I knew it
that September night
            in Amsterdam.
And having been without love
for so long a time
and what new knowledge
each encounter brings
I must have been
as ready as the rose is
to be caressed
and then be ruined
      by the rain.

THE FIRST WEEK

HOTEL De L'EUROPE, WINTER: EARLY EVENING

Cold. The window open, curtains spread as far apart as they will go. Outside, the sky dominates everything. Because I haven't closed the window yet, my bed is now so full of moon there's almost no room left in it for me. What a bed this is. What a wide, soft Dutch bed this old hotel has given me this time to lie in by myself.

In a city like Amsterdam if you sleep alone, you do so by choice. But after all the nights, good, bad, indifferent, not different I'd rather stay here empty inside/outside than bed down just to bed down. I've been more alone when someone wrong was here than I've been when no one came. Still . . . Never mind, if I don't get up to close the window now there'll be no sleep at all.

I will not chase the shadows any more. I'll draw the curtains tight and sleep. I'll work. I'll read. I'll go to sleep.

LATER ON

I wake up. Wondering, not knowing where I am. What time is it? Where am I? Geographically, Holland. In my thoughts and in my head I am no place. No where that I have been before. I am away, that much is so. Nothing is familiar. But it has been this way for some days now.

I pass by mirrors and walk with my reflection, go out into the cold Dutch night and see my breath before me, buy things and pay for them with money from the bottom part of my jeans, elicit smiles and sometimes get them back, write my name and see it on the page in front of me, throw popcorn to those few brave birds who still brave winter. People not known to me recognize me and so I am.

I participate, act out, think. All these things are tangibles, done, seen by me. I am alive. I function.

If I sleep the wrong way and wake up knotted, I feel the pain. I drink too much and the headache every other morning is real. It takes the same time going as it always did. I caught my finger in the door a week ago and the swelling hasn't yet gone down. Though it almost never rings, I answer the telephone and hear myself speak. Proof that I'm alive. I react, I have reactions.

But I am not here, as sure as I am not in Boston or driving through Detroit with Jack.

I cannot discern how long I've been away or if I'm still in transport. I might be on the edge of dying or living. Clearly I am on the edge.

SATURDAY NOON

Here now the maple trees
ejaculating in the fall wind.
They'll be bare in only hours
while the wind not even breathless
will rape and rampage
      on the higher hills.

Such an effortless excess,
those light limbs letting go,
but given the wind's full passion,
what willow would not
                bend to it?

The pines sweep down
the sky's broad bottom
uninterrupted by the fog
and not bedazzled by the rain,

Each a many-fingered broom
not pretending to be stately
more uncommon or more useful
                than a simple broom.

SATURDAY NIGHT

To see them dance
is always such a marvel
whether they run down
the length of Strauss
or stand in place for *Stoney End.*

Their motions are as fluid
as a kind of liquid neon,
even on a floor so crowded
that each of them appears
to be the other's
next of kin.

The dancing
like the darkness
has no starting place
and seemingly no real end.

If you come here
three nights running
you begin to feel
the night starts only
with your arrival
and stops as quickly
when you go.

I wasn't dancing
but I wasn't standing still.
I wasn't hunting, but I hoped.
New Year's Eve did not fill up
the forefront of my mind.
I didn't need tomorrow
                  only now.

Maybe I stayed longer
            than I'd planned
for with the music
and the lateness of the hour
before I'd finished living *now*
I was driving through tomorrow.

Later on the street
the last fall leaves
were flying through
                    the railings
to float
      along
          the dark
                  canal.

Another evening maybe:
with the winter dead ahead
I had three dozen nights
lined up and waiting
no different than the one
I'd just come through.

I could be content
to walk back slowly
and finally slide down into
that same safe security
that only hotel beds afford.

Knowing that it waited
empty in the darkness,
my footsteps quickened.

SUNDAY NIGHT

I'm living,
no I'm *staying*,
down the street.
We can walk.

MONDAY AFTERNOON

Blinking like an owl in morning
I woke up wanting you,
for all the Denver days ahead
              and ever after.
for all the Sausalitos past
and Boston nights that ended
before they had beginnings.

Thick throated still
and not yet
              wide awake enough
I finally came alive
to find you studying me.

I wish that I
had told you then
I wasn't what you watched,
and given time to rearrange
my face and frame for you,
I'd be closer to the man
who picked you up
            the night before.
Nearer to whatever
you must have wanted
or expected.

But seeing you
at my breath's edge
filled my head
with such a wonder
that I could only
pray in silence
that though your eyes
                    were open
you stared at me from sleep.
A sleep I wouldn't dare
                    invade.

TUESDAY AFTERNOON

A cat
came off the higher roof
and down below my window,
balancing on so thin a rail
that even pigeons had not dared
that tightrope walk before.

A red and yellow cat
            of some age
and some experience
sat the afternoon out
down below my window—waiting
as he must have known
    I waited.
A cat for company
until the sunset started
then he leisurely climbed back.

TUESDAY NIGHT

I don't know why we lie here
on the floor collecting dust
when both of us are well aware
that any bed's more comfortable
than carpet over hardwood.
What the evening needs
            is some suggestion.
One of us will have to stop
being or pretending to be shy.

Till boldness catches hold,
of you or me or we,
use my elbow as a pillow
let my body cover you
        as lightly as it can
with this bumpy body blanket.

Now we're eye to eye. Hello.

WEDNESDAY

I move in close,
        crouching
           like a fighter
waiting for a chance.
      An opening.

I cannot wait much longer.
Give in quietly or go.

Are you that wild
late-blooming plant?
If so you must not wait
             to tell me
for there's little time
within this life
      and the next one's
          nearly spent.

WEDNESDAY NIGHT

I don't have to touch you
to be touching you
nor feel your face
to feel your face.
Yet sometimes touching you
I feel you not at all.

There seems to be
so much of you at times
        enough to fill
and spill across the room.
Other times
I stretch in your direction
and draw back to me
great armfuls of nothing,
great handfuls of air.

THURSDAY

Bicycle bells
and barrel organs
bellowing through
the bedroom window
woke me early,
though I had been awake
an hour before,
closing my arm about you
while you barely stirred,
avoiding my face in sleep
the way new lovers always do
the first night in
the first night out.

Then sleeping again,
        at least I did,
until half-opened eyes
let me observe you
dressing in that same
thick silence
that in the end
surrounded us
        the night before.

Perhaps I fell asleep again
or closed my eyes
    for one long minute—
moments later
when I opened them again
you'd finished dressing
and were gone.

THURSDAY AFTERNOON

I bought red dahlias
           for you
and sunflowers
from across the square.
They have not yet
begun to fall.

THURSDAY EVENING

Goodbye.
I know no other way
          to say it.
What shall I call you?
             Never mind.
This poem is for you
and you will know it
in Munich or in Minnesota.

It only complicates
my life as well as yours
to set your name down here
as well as detail
inch by inch the night.

The windmills turn
and we turn too,
not with the wind
but slowly,
imperceptibly away.

Not noticed by the sunset,
        if there is one
or by anyone.
Not we ourselves.

We will not walk again
along canals together.
And the record player
will not play *We Will*.

It's somehow miracle enough
that Amstel beer in Amsterdam
made us drunk enough
to meet at all.

Still,
September
has a way with it
        and a way
of coming round
next year
and the next year too.

And Thursday comes around
at least once every week.

FRIDAY

How right to love you,
across the room
across the seas
and if need be
all across a lifetime
with you or without you.

Your going is a fact,
your taking leave
with but a telephoned goodbye
        almost a certainty.

I'll gain no understanding
from your absence
and any truth I fall upon
by my own hand
would have met me sooner
had you been beside me
to attract and guide it
down our double road.

FRIDAY AFTERNOON

I wish I had a camera
to photograph the sunflowers.
Seven of them still alive
staring at the ceiling
as if the sun shone there.

THE SECOND WEEK

SATURDAY MORNING

And now
the table's bloody
with red petals.
The sunflowers too
begin to sag.

I have paced
            these rooms
and rolled alone
upon this bed
two dozen times today.

I've been out walking
and come back
and been out walking
            once again.

The street was empty
till ten-thirty.
Now it's filling up.
It seems as though
all Amsterdam
has the morning off.

My watch is running fast
or my watch is running slow.
One or the other is the truth,
I'm removed from any sense
                    of real time.

For the better part
of this one week
I've set my timepiece
by your coming
and your going.
My only clock now
is the chiming
in the square.

My sense of distance
          hasn't changed.
I still feel miles
and worlds away
from anything that was
                    or is.

More and more
I wonder if that distance
always was and has been
as compatible as closeness.

If this is so,
the habit must be changed
or tempered by a truth
so new or revolutionary
that it's not yet evident,
not laid out or shown to me
for what it is or should be.

If I'm to be a man
of dark distance
        set apart
from what I thought I needed,
then the distance has to be
a metered, measured one.

SUNDAY MORNING

Soon the tulips
will come shooting
through the earth's first thaw.
There'll be no Holland winter
to keep me locked inside
                    what then?

What of the promises
filtered through the rain
digested out of so much snow
that they drift aimlessly
down every gutter?

And you?
On the street again
        and sleeveless.
Do you troll for strangers
each alike to you
or to your liking?
In what country, please.
In what land.

I deserve the punishment
                of knowing
for having come to know you.

Even with the thaw
I can't as yet
bring myself to slip
among the narrow streets
or venture down the block
to buy new cheese and apples.

I'm afraid and sure
that all eyes know
you went away
or didn't come at all.
You were. But never were.

Couldn't you have left
                    a wristwatch
a damp slip hanging
in the bathroom?
Couldn't you have sent a postcard
                    a photograph?

Where was the courtesy
on that dark winter morning
demanding that you slide
a sealed envelope
beneath my door
that when opened
might have said
the single final word.

Goddamn you
for your lack of etiquette
that doesn't let me show off
               even to myself
the sureness of goodbye.
Proof these months
of slow self-pity
were caused by the death
of something that had lived.

THE SECOND MONDAY

Far off, nothing.
And I expect
if it were
later in the day
even that semi-sure,
too near horizon
would blur into
a single blue,
the color of
    cheap china.

Being near the sea
has stalled the coming
of some madness
I'll meet later.
How long I keep it
at a distance
depends to some extent
upon what solace
I get from this ocean.

Truth is never absolute
as lies are seldom ever
              lies completely.
No one ever seems to notice
or even try to take apart
that gray matter
lurking in between the two.

If there is
a universal truth
it lies within the certainty
that no one really listens,
not even to the radio
or the radiator's bumping.

People hear all right
but only those few things
a lifelong, built-in scrambler
will let pass through.
Any hope of other thoughts
getting through the maze
          is like a quest
without a consequence
or a journey started out,
meant to have no end.

TWO MONTHS LATER

MONDAY, TWO MONTHS LATER

Now I have the time
to take you riding
        in the car
to lie with you
in private deserts
or eat with you
in public restaurants.

Now I have the time
for football all fall long
and to apologize
for little lies and big lies
told when there was no time
to explain the truth.

I am finished
with whatever tasks
kept me from walking
in the woods with you
            or leaping
in the Zanford sand.

I have so much time
that I can build for you
sand castles out of mortar.

Midweek picnics.
Minding my temper in traffic.
Washing your back
and cleaning out my closets.
Staying in bed with you
long past the rush hour
and the pangs of hunger
and listening to the story
                of your life
in deadly detail.
Whatever time it takes,
I have that time.

I'd hoped that I might
take you traveling
down the block
or to wherever.

I've always wanted
to watch flowers open
all the way,
however long
the process took.

Now I have the time
to be bored
to be delivered
to be patient
to be understanding,
to give you
all the time you need.

Now I have the time.
      Where are you?

POSTLUDE

Leaving Again

1.

A phrase of love
can be strung out
in such a way
that *hate* by contrast
sounds more beautiful.

Canaries do not sing love,
and the truest lovers
cannot always say love's name
but by their actions
they speak volumes
yet unpublished and
as yet not written down.

Love stings
when it should tingle
and leaves long scars
instead of
    deep impressions.

Worst of all
for love gone wrong
there is no warranty
or bond to cover damage.

The guarantee
for finding sanity again
is finding love again
and giving over
to the new beloved
that one facet of yourself
you held back last time.

If it should happen to you
one more time,
        and it will,
display your love
in all its Sunday clothes
for unless you go out
with your face held high
toward the sunlight
how are you to know?

2.

Why is it
that in some far place,
away from home
and true or trumped-up
            responsibility
we are so willing
to volunteer everything?

In doing so
I do suppose
we offer nothing.
No thing that those
of like persuasions
might hitch up to.

How many empty rooms
around the world
does it finally take
to prove that to us?

I am not alone
in letting go
and I am not unique
        in giving in.

Others take advantage
of that month
or two-week span
called vacation or escape.

In truth that time
is just enough reality
to get us through
the other forty-eight
or fifty weeks.

3.

Today I crossed
the corridors of hell
and paced my way
         through purgatory
and so my hour in heaven
        should be assured.

Stand still,
I hear me saying
        to myself
and all the while
my legs keep moving,
as if they hadn't
        exercised enough.
As if they needed practice
for some journey yet to come.

Intermission

And we go on
still we go on
and we go on
you can see us go on . . .
McKuen

APRIL FIFTH, 9:22 A.M.

Just now an earthquake moves beneath me. Even as it ends, another shudder shakes the ground. A California fact. An anniversary almost of that quake two, three years ago that jostled me from bed at six and set the dogs to howling and caused a crack to run eye level down the front room stairs.

I cannot be shaken up. If I could I'd sway more willingly than most and go whichever way the earth or some mover of the earth thought I should go.

I've had my first inside the world and felt for sure I was its axis. I've seen the kings go by, though I'll admit my vantage point was from some distance. For derring-do I've sailed through clouds more easily than I once floated on a pond. However jerry-built my life has been, I've felt there was solidity of sorts. In truth there is, however little. I built what I though needed building— some would say security, I'd still say solidity for some one.

There must have been a blueprint once. Now, no trace of any master plan remains, as nobody stops or stays here still.

I do not brood. I am not malcontent. I am not. Where once I had opinions good and bad of what I'd done. Even to myself. I have no opinions now.

It, whatever that should be or is, is over, never started or never was. What I do have is this life, half built—unfinished. Selfish though I can be, it was never made for me. There are takers, just that. But, as I go out, there is no one here or up ahead that I can give it to.

I wonder how long I can move, go through the motions, knowing what I know. How many years or days are left. Why go through the motions anyway?

I don't know.

Mexico, A House By The Sea—1974

**For Us, Whoever We Are
And for W. T.**

He heals all wounds
who takes away my life.

MICHELANGELO

WHAT OF THE OCEAN

What of the ocean? Why the pull for me of sea beneath blue sky? I am surely not a Merman, a duck within some other life. Nor willingly would I be sailor, leaving land too long a time. I could not live the life of some far fisherman, hip-high in water every morning, pulling in the nets at night.

Something tugs at me, I've no doubt of that. Something from the sea, whichever one I'm near. And when I stray too far from beachland I'm called back. I do not know what calls or carries me till I'm within the range of water once again. I do know that the calm times, the quiet ones— not necessarily the best—are lived out by me near the sea. By myself.

No man wants the hidden hand of anything to be his pilot. Some journeys he should set out on with only maps of his own choosing; no compass but the one he carries in his head, then when he sails past the earth's edge that will be only his own business.

More than I love anything or anyone within my realm and capability of loving, I love the sea. So I go seaward once again or I'm pulled back, whatever.

BEACH DIARY

The sun full measured
this second day
of this fourth year
of coming back
   and coming back
and coming back again
         to Mexico.

In the trees it crouches now
        until it springs out
harsher than remembered
to bake me through the noon.

Siestas notwithstanding
the heat has got them all
impatient, amorous
                    or ambitious.

Lizards in the patio
squaring off at either end
then racing down the tile
toward each other,
hind ends reared
and hind legs stiffened,
they snap and scatter
in the dance of courtship.

In the end
      like movie dinosaurs
they clash and roll
in twisted knots
the balance of the afternoon.

Having seen the ritual
acted out and realized
I started back to sleep
beneath the kindest weather
that I've known
        in twenty months.

Suddenly they're in the hedge.
Rustling, threading through
                the roots,
Tunneling
in the dead leaf carpeting.

                Whoosh,
and one comes flying
through the thicket
like an alligator given wings.

Later
when the sun
starts slumping seaward
it will be the gulls' turn
to file through the air
in bad formation.

Not as agile as the sparrows
(as near P38s as any bird)
nor as graceful as wild geese
jetting home at spring,
these troop transport gulls
                    are clumsy.

Fuel tanks full
you can almost see
their sleep beginning
as they fly, no, stumble by.

Sand crabs again
         scrambling sideways
dragging unbelievable burdens
through the soft red sunset.
A fish head gorged up by a gull
twice the sand crab's size.
Another darts off easily
with half a clam.

My long shadow passing past them
is enough to send these recluses
down their well-dug holes.

Could I invade
this spider diary
I might turn up
the seashore chronicle
of one whole winter
or at the very least
a pattern more elaborate
than the tank-like tracks
of a thousand sand crabs
invading that first atoll
past and all along
                    the shoreline.

Evening
and a single gecko's
loud percussion
heard above the waves
          above the wind
above the crickets,
not yet chorusing
but making ready.

Geckos everywhere.
Between the roof beams
along the stuccoed wall
above the arch
of every doorway.

A dozen now. More.
Pale off-white in color
        almost yellow.
Only slightly darker
than the once white plaster.
Hanging on,
upside down and sideways.
Not moving, not sleeping.
Geckos. Not like crystal.
Not hard like alabaster.
More like marzipan.
Fragile looking.

They sound again.
The echo through the arches
                    could be one or five.
Castanets in double time.

I half expect
that Spanish dancers
will come bursting through the door,
vests and petticoats of every color
heels stomping, snapping, clicking
ready for some fine fiesta.

Stars.
A few are falling.
No comet yet,
but it's expected.

The day
has opened up,
progressed and gone.
I've watched it move
from the lizard's lost siesta
to Don Quixote of La Mancha's
imagined but not held
                    fiesta.

FISHERMEN

Brown fishermen
have reaped their harvest
one more day
    and now head slowly home,
half a truckload of them.

Legs dangling
from the back end of a pickup
their eyes not leaving
that long white line
that crawls out evenly below them.

The cough
and sputter truck
hugs the shoulder
of the mountain road
climbing slower
as the hill gets higher.

Faster cars wait, honk
grumble back behind it
in a head to taillight line.
Then chancing
            on the widest curve
sail by at racetrack speed.

Still mute and mesmerized
by tiredness
      and that white stripe
brown fishermen head home.

A POSTCARD, WEDNESDAY

A card. You're coming down. I half expected it, but didn't hope. I don't know if I'm glad. I want to be. But for some ten days now, no visitor has come or gone. I admit that I've not thought of you so very much. I've been content to live these days as they arrive.

I wonder what it is that you expect from me. What is it that I want from you? I used to know, if I thought about it. Maybe that was it. I never thought about it. No time to think just now, you're coming down.

This afternoon I'll drive into the city, buy fresh fruit, canned juices and some bread. Eggs. The farmer down the road has fresh ones . . . I'm glad the car is working well. I'll wait and let you straighten up the bedroom. Rearrange the furniture, but don't rearrange my life.

I refuse, and this is just for me to know, to measure every word this time. To think and think again before reacting to a passage said aloud from whatever book you're reading. I will not close or open up my thoughts with prudence or premeditation.

I must be me again, especially in front of you. Lately I've been tracking forward and tracing back, looking to see who I am. I am me. That isn't much but it's a start. Somewhere, some time ago, whenever—you must have wanted me. Or why did we begin? Surely you know clay is easier to come by than a half-grown man, simpler to bend to what you want than someone's back that's nearly straight.

I'm already made. Too much living has gone on within this shell for it to change. Not indifferent to being made different, I'm merely bored at any thought of being changed. I'll bend. You know I will. But it's a curiosity that with each year that passes, my back gets straighter, stronger still.

Yes, I'm glad you're coming. Though it makes a ripple in the ocean, I might find out if I'm as good a sailor as I think and hope I am.

REINTRODUCTION

You're here.

Seeing you
the second time
makes me feel
I had my eyes closed
when we met before.

Yes
the *whole* of it
would be the best.
All pretense
not pretended any more.

But you are here.
That is enough for you
and by necessity for now
      enough for me.

      You're here.
What happens in this moment,
even if it's nothing,
      is enough.

REALITY, VERSUS...

What goes on unseen
untold to us
    by one the other
is more real
than all the sentences
our senses spoke
        and speak.

I see your face and know
a tilting of your shoulder
speaks whole paragraphs aloud
whole stories filled with proof
that what is happening
is if anything a willful lie
both of us indulge in.

This much is fact.
You do not amaze me
with your dark indifference
You never once astound me
by being only what
I wish you to be.

I await the crumbs
        just now
delighted that they come
from bread lifted out of ovens
by some hidden master baker.

FLASHBACK, BOSTON

Your back is to me and I'm only half asleep. Things fuse. People start to be that one you always half expect. There haven't been so many, but as years go on you isolate those qualities you wanted from the ones you didn't want and chisel them the way a sculptor would into a perfect mass. Not a statue but a someone bending your own way and bending you to theirs.

New England? If not then take a compliment, for that full face and body met and living there needs no addition or subtraction to be as perfect as perfection is.

If it was not you, blue-white eyes framed by wire spectacles, that brought me from across the room, then allow me to imagine back. Don't interrupt my thinking and I'll not interfere as you sleep up the sun.

I remember that I looked away in wonder, that it happened, that I had proof of it, that spring is all that everyone, including me, has said it is.

Will I one day rephrase, reappraise the Boston spring that handed you over to me? You for two days only, one on your ground, one on mine, a third split down the middle. Am I to have the luxury—for luxury, read time—to find out if you really are as you really are or do I go on definitely/indefinitely seeing in my head only your thighs inside/outside mine?

Let me come back. Let us both come back. I'll pole-vault high, clear through the middle of your mattress next time and pull myself straight into you. Even winded after all the stairs, you'll know I'm there. Wait for me. Keep the window open and your tooth-gap smile alive a while longer. Just a small while. I won't be long.

No elevators leading to high rooms and canopied beds in old hotels, we'll stay and be in your room only or walk the whole of Boston in a single afternoon or one long endless evening.

NORTH STREET REMEMBERED

You'll have a phonograph
            a chef's hat
and a yellow suit
of your own choosing,
even if we have to
pay for them on time.
A canopy above the bed
that I can chin on.
A headboard
you can prop your head against
            and
                    read.

You can write and polish words
while I sit quietly
            in some dark corner
                        watching.

I'll teach you music
slowly and without pain
and you can show me
how to make a Quiche Lorraine.

I've never been up Beacon Hill,
            you can take me there.
Later in the summer
we'll go to that beach
in Provincetown.
You can show me
where you started
writing out your poem.

Don't you see
I've got it all worked out
we'll follow every sun
        there is to follow.
We'll be equal in all things
you'll give me youth and you
I'll give you more of me
        than I yet know.
Each other we will give
        each other's other.

I'll lose weight, you'll see.
Before we leave for California
                Paris or wherever
we'll get it all together.

I never sleep so well
as when I'm sleeping
           next to you
or talk so much
as when I'm talking
      at your ear.
My hand
while touching
just your back
has touched the sky
as sure as God has groped
          the stars.

Ask my name
and it's now yours.
Demand my purpose
and you know it's you.
My needs are only
those wants you want.
And when I sleep this night
          or any after this,
though you be miles gone,
my head still rests
against your belly,
          moving down.
Or at your back
against your shoulders
moving not at all.

IN CASE YOU DIDN'T KNOW

Some days up ahead
will come down empty
and some years fuller
than the fullest one
we've known before.

Today has been
the best day yet.
　　　　I thought
you ought to know that,
and I thought it time
that I said *thank you*
for whatever might have
passed between us
that in your mind
you might have felt
missed my attention.

It didn't
and it doesn't
and it won't.

Thank you
for the everydays
that you make
       into holidays.

I close up
more often now,
not just to you
but even to myself
            within myself.

I know I should
be always open.
At least I ought to make
            a better try.

I will.

HAD I THE COURAGE OF ONE

Such distance there is
between your back
and this new morning.

Had I the courage of one
I'd turn you around.
Had I the courage of five
I'd turn around inside you
pulling all the dark earth
                  with me.

Had I the courage of ten
we'd start so much together
that we'd never have the time
to finish even one thing started.

Had I the courage of one hundred
I'd stand back and look at you.
                    That's all.

Moving away, moving away,
gone you are while yet arriving.
Had I the courage of one
I'd run beside you or behind you.

Instead I run away.
So it is we've started out
on this new day together
to travel parallel paths
in opposite directions.

FRIDAY WALK

This morning's walk produced no shells of any great variety, though the beach was up and about its daily business. Sand dollars, finding themselves naked on the shore slide into sand like flying saucers burrowing in the earth, caught in an alien country and forced to hide. I shook a hermit crab from the one shell I'd decided I should salvage. Another sand crab drilled deep to set up housekeeping, beneath a great bloated fish washed up on the shore some days before and now grown fatter in the sea air and the sun.

I believe that more and more the sea rejects what it finds useless or how could I explain still more twisted driftwood drenched and shriveling in this same Mexican sun that inflates that now unflinching fish.

INNER WORKINGS

I have seen you
when your smiles and frowns
were so tied up and intermingled
that none—not even you
could have said
with any sureness
what face you were giving
        to the crowd.

I have walked with you to subways
when parting was difficult
and less than twenty minutes later
been with someone else
and loved you none the less.

I have spied on you
and looked accusingly,
when I, myself, knew well
that I was in the wrong.

I have wept for you,
                    about you
and one time with you.
I have shared your secrets
and kept private
secrets of my own.

I have fought with you
and over you,
loved you and disliked you
in equal parts
and at the same time.

I have thought
that I would die
if you failed to turn up
on some pre-selected night
and when you didn't—
                    wished I would.

I have loved you
never asking if I should.
I have trusted you
not caring if I could
        or couldn't.

In company
with strangers or your friends
I have smiled and gone on smiling
when I thought no single smile
                        or grin
was yet left inside me.

If we were unhappy
with one the other
why shouldn't it be
            just our concern?

I have watched you play
with other people's children
and felt they were our own.

I've heard you hum
some made-up tune at breakfast
and watched you killing time all day
while you awaited killing me at night.

I have lied to you
for no good reason.
I have troubled you
and even when I knew it
sometimes that didn't make me stop.

The things we do
in love's name
never stop surprising me.
I'm amazed that love
can live at all
through all the subterfuge,
pass through all the barricades,
stumble over all the obstacles
we construct and put up
            in its way.

That first seed
wherever planted
must have been a hearty strain.

Just now
what kind of passion
stirs inside me
      I can't say.
I feel for you
and it's as much as love
but whether it's because
I feel you leaving,
slipping from me day by day
or because I need, depend on,
                  want just you
I have no way of knowing.

Our lives together
have become so knotted,
                    muddled up
that who's to say
            where the heart ended
and habit started in to open up?

I love you—yes
But I don't mean for you
                    to know it.

MORNING COLLECTION

Seeking
more important treasures
than the common clam shell
every tide gives up,
I've been out collecting
bits of driftwood and debris
for your dresser top.

A conch from which I shook
an irritated hermit crab.
A half-pint rum bottle
              I collected,
some shells and stones
        of no importance.

Starfish, white
against the whiter sand
(I sailed the pink ones—
limp and living still)
back into the sea.
Probably I'll find them
here again tomorrow,
midway through
        my morning walk.

The sea gives up the living
as it does the recent dead,
at will it casts off
                what it will.

Morning people
tracking down the shore
retrieve the best
and see the very worst
the sea sheds on the beach.

MONDAY BEACH

Take a picture of me,
     fat and brown.
So that I'll remember
how I looked
from the outside
when I knew within
that by my own hand
I had started systematically
to take my life.

But my life
is bought and paid for.
It does not belong to you
            or God,
or any man now drawing breath.
I am free to give it as a whole
to any ocean of my liking
or dismantle it in private
            piece by piece
by pills or poetry,
the poison of just letting go
or any other means
        I think befitting
    of the public hero
            and the private coward.

THE TIME COMES

Finally the time comes.
        Irrevocably.
Never the same way twice.
And the going isn't easy.

Each tries to make the other
        think the blame belongs
exclusively to him.
And so it does.

I hardly even tried,
I'm past the point of that.
How could I presume to finalize
what maybe never should have been.

I started in
not knowing who I am
when was it, never mind.
I dwell too much on me.

Still now we don't know
          one the other
and that's as good a way
          to end as start.

There is nothing
you or me
or either one of us
          can say.
Beyond hello before goodbye
          there should be
a sting of words
or one long paragraph
to make the ending easy.

I'm so amazed
at finding out
my head still reels
under even friendly blows
that I'm determined
not to let the boxer
          or the battler
come in close again

Nor will I willingly go out
into the evening any more
and place myself within
that enchanted circle
          of the hunters.
The moving staircase
          or the rain.

I have so little permanency
and not much time left up ahead
I ought to stay at home
behind the iron gates
          and rainbow glass.
Sure places I've constructed.

It's quiet there
          and best of all
the disappointments yet to come
can be lived by me in private.
No one need ever know
if the wounds are fatal
or if I'm waiting out some healing time.

There is an emptiness
and it is deep.
A wound so old
that healing wouldn't work.

If I have not yet
come back around
to where I started
then I am only inches
from that now narrow
                corridor
that will bring me there.

Relief I feel,
I'll not deny it.
But there's a sorrow too
as though the world was finally
slipping from me and away.

Perspective, I have none.
Sorrow—there isn't any.
Plans? What plans could I have
except to live here for a time
until I know it's finally time
                              to go.

THE AIRPORT ROAD

Look.
The first sail that we've seen
            and it comes closer.

I didn't tell you
but this morning when I took my sea walk
small fish were flopped up
all along the shore.
Gills muddy and still gasping
there were too many to throw back.

Four or five Mexican children
were running and laughing
popping them into baskets.

They went away with baskets full
                    and overflowing,
laughing still and happy.

Come back if you have reason to,
or hunt me up wherever.
Be careful on the airport road
it's being paved again
and even if it wasn't
no one down here drives
                    with any certainty.

Write me.
Yes, write me.
The Acapulco news
is all I get here
and the L. A. *Times*
if I go into town—
but you know all of that.
Be careful on the airport road.

I'm glad you came to visit me.

THE FIRST

No matter when I start
that first day's walk
along the tide's white ragged edge,
someone's been ahead of me.

I went at noon the first day,
              ten the next.
Finally at sunrise
I started out
and on this very morning
I was up before the sun
guided by the whitecaps only
luminous in the dimming starlight.

When at last the light
began to rim the far horizon
I saw beside my own, new footprints
in the Monday sand
a larger imprint trailing on
                    ahead of me.
And beside that wide stride
on this quiet beach
the soft impression of a dog
who must have trotted
by his master's side.

I've but one more morning
left to me
before I trade Tres Vidas
                for the city,
but if I have to start out
down the beach at midnight
                    or before
I'm determined to confront
that brown beach man
who dares to think
he loves my ocean
more than me.

And anyway,
the ocean's all
that I have left.
There won't be anyone again,
but there will always be
sea water and sea things
to wash the memories
            into one another.

That's a comfort
not to be taken lightly.
considering the sea
            is all I have.

THE END OF JANUARY

The ocean rumbles on. Wave after wave, one over the other, faster than the preceding wave recedes. On the far horizon, nothing. As far as I can see at either end, nothing.

There was a small rain this morning. No trace of it now, not on shore or sea. A school—or at most, half a dozen sharks zigzagged back and forth when the sea was calmer. Earlier a man walked down the beach. Never bending. Not stopping. Not collecting.

Far into January we are. Almost at the end. The comet didn't come. I watched some nights, got up early several mornings, but if a comet came or went or stays above me I failed to pick it out from all the other stars. Stars there are at night, aplenty.

Getting back to days, as each one deepens a breeze and then a wind grows more intense. I have said what there is to say. Described what I, myself, have seen. Beyond that, there is nothing. Nothing in abundance.

I do not accuse. There is no blame to place. Nothing's wrong. It's just that nothing's right.

I won't pretend that Holland was the starting point, for something that has started and now stops. Anyway, the Netherlands seem so many dozen years away. I can't explain Mexico as any more than what it is. Mexico. Boston begins, and is over, on one long weekend.

If I knew why I had the need to travel out of my own room, my space, to anywhere, I might be able to explain what's gone or isn't coming.

There are half a hundred sentences unfinished, unstarted on these pages. And as this out of season summer rolls beneath me and away, I wait. The mystery of the sea's no clearer than it was for me before. Worse, the mystery of myself grows harder to discern.

I am waiting. I will do so, while I can.

ABOUT THE AUTHOR

ROD MCKUEN was born in Oakland, California, and has traveled extensively throughout the world as both a concert artist and a writer. In less than six years his books of poetry have sold over nine million copies in hard-cover, making him the best-selling and most widely read poet of all time, as well as the best-selling living author writing in any hard-cover medium today. His poetry is taught and studied in schools, colleges, universities and seminaries all over the world, and the author spends a good deal of his time visiting and lecturing on campuses.

Mr. McKuen is also the composer of more than 1,000 songs that have been translated into Spanish, French, Dutch, German, Russian, Czechoslovakian, Japanese, Chinese, Norwegian and Italian, among other languages. They account for the sale of more than one hundred million records. His film music has twice been nominated for Motion Picture Academy Awards.

Rod McKuen's classical music, including symphonies, concertos, piano sonatas and his very popular Adagio for Harp & Strings, is performed by leading orchestras in the United States and throughout Europe. In May of 1972, the Royal Philharmonic Orchestra in London premiered his Concerto #3 for Piano & Orchestra, and an orchestral suite, The Plains of My Country. In October 1973, the Louisville Orchestra premiered Mr. McKuen's latest commissioned work, The City, which was nominated for a Pulitzer Prize in music in 1974. His newest commissions include music and lyrics for a multi-media ballet presented by Nicholas Petrov and the Pittsburgh Ballet as part of the Bicentennial celebration in 1976.

Before becoming a best-selling author and composer, Mr. McKuen worked as a laborer, radio disc jockey and newspaper columnist. From 1953 to 1955, he served in the army in Japan and Korea.